RALEIGH
A Guide to
North Carolina's Capital

Published by The Raleigh Fine Arts Society, Inc.

The Raleigh Fine Arts Society was organized in 1965 "To further art in the community .... and encourage public appreciation, enthusiasm, support, and understanding of art, music, and literature."

—from Articles of Incorporation of
The Raleigh Fine Arts Society, Inc.

The Raleigh Fine Arts Society has financed the publication of this book with the assistance of a grant from the North Carolina Arts Council.

The North Carolina Arts Council, a state agency, is a section of the Division of the Arts, North Carolina Department of Cultural Resources. It was established in 1964 to assist in the cultural growth of all North Carolinians by promoting the arts at the community level, the term "arts" taken to include architecture and the visual environment, crafts, dance, drama, literature, music, painting, sculpture, photography, film, and the public media. The council welcomes communication by mail (North Carolina Arts Council, N. C. Department of Cultural Resources, Raleigh, 27611) or by telephone (919/829-7897).

Foreword

It was the hope of the Raleigh Fine Arts Society that this guide would remain current for at least five years. Alas! We can't type fast enough to keep up with the changes in Raleigh, and parts of the book may be out of date before the ink dries. The Capitol itself overlooks a rapidly changing scene with construction of both the Fayetteville Street Mall and the state's Bicentennial Plaza underway. The State Government Mall, which will extend north from the Legislative Building, will further alter the area north of the Capitol.

Although several structures have been moved to make way for new streets, other well-loved buildings standing in the way of progress face possible demolition. Many of those left are shabby relics of better days; however, we don't apologize for them—we're grateful for their continued existence.

So take a fast look at your guidebook and let us, unequivocally and without fear of change, bid you welcome to the capital city. Since Raleigh was occupied by Sherman's troops and one of his men wrote, "Perhaps there is no town of the same population in the South that affords so many evidences of wealth, intelligence, enterprise, elegance, and social refinement," visitors have acclaimed Raleigh's beauty and hospitality. These, we hope, will never change.

Alexa Carroll Williams, Editor
Ann Vallentyne Walker, Chairman
Ann Brower Turner, President
The Raleigh Fine Arts Society, Inc.

Raleigh: somewhat better than someplace else ...

In 1957, when I came to Raleigh to live and work, I crept up on the city in the early morning, riding the roller coaster of wooded hills along U. S. 70 from the west.

It was wilderness all the way right up to the Carolina Country Club. Meadowlarks and mourning doves walked in the dew of the dawn. A fawn darted across the highway.

Raleigh was still "Old Raleigh," then a city of some 80,000 souls just stirring themselves from Blount Street aristocracy into a budding, bustling city which had its heart on Fayetteville Street where at the staid, historic "Sir Walter" hotel debutantes danced til dawn and politicians met in smoke-filled rooms to name governors and senators and plot their mischief against the unsuspecting public.

A new city has replaced the old. Raleigh now rushes out half way to Durham to greet you. Though the Capitol is still the sentimental center of the city, traffic runs away from it. Fayetteville Street, still pronounced "Fedville" in symbolic slaughter of the language of the French who gave us the Marquis de la Fayette who in turn helped us win the Revolution, is the main drag in name only.

Raleigh, pronounced "Rolly," was named for that English gentleman of like name. But we take the word of Nell Styron, local journalist and descendant of an "Old Rawleigh" family, who once warned us: "Don't let anyone tell you that Sir Walter Raleigh came over with the Lost Colony. He was a handsome man. He never got to Carolina. Queen Elizabeth saw to that."

Every few years we talk about erecting a monument to that romantic rogue. But the nearest we got to that was a statue carved out of a cypress tree. The sculptor said we could have it for free. But nobody thanked him so he packed it up, left town and I imagine some other city with no right to it is going to put it on its town square.

Unlike Sandburg's city of "hog butcher and wheat stacker," Raleigh is more "pencil pusher" and "deep thinker" with its canyons of state offices and its sprawling green acres of college campus.

Climate-wise, Raleigh is hot in summer, warm in winter. Snows are rare but fully appreciated. Schools close at the drop of a flake, much to the chagrin of our Yankee newcomers who ridicule the natives for their fear of driving in ice and snow and who cleverly disguise their New England accents when they call the tow truck to pull them out of the ditch.

No prettier town is to be found. In the springtime, with the woodland white with dogwood bending gently over red and pink azaleas, Raleigh is a bridesmaid on her way to a wedding of God and nature. Autumn finds her gowned in gold and red enroute to a football game, a picnic in the park, a play or concert in the town.

A newcomer, who described Raleigh as a nice bedroom community with no city to be a bedroom to, said it with envy in his voice, admitting it's a "nice place to settle down in, live in, and die in."

Most strangers get to feel that way in short time. Yet some of them leave by choice, others by necessity. And some look back in scorn or pretended anger, coming home to rummage through attics and closets, looking for skeletons that might well fit into a prize-winning short story or a best seller. But after the royalties are in and the relatives reassured, they usually add a postscript that while Raleigh ain't Eden, it's about as close to it as any crossroads town in America.

And many of us share the anxiety of the elderly Raleigh citizen who, when finally called to Paradise, wondered wistfully as she went: "Do you reckon it will be anything like Raleigh?"

Certainly we hope so.

A. C. Snow

A. C. Snow is editor of the *Raleigh Times*.

The Unalterable Capital

Raleigh didn't just happen; the city was planned by the state and built on land in Wake County near Wake Crossroads, or Bloomsbury, to become the "unalterable capital of North Carolina."

When Wake County, close to the geographical center of the state, was chosen as the site for the state's permanent capital, it was stipulated that the specific location be within 10 miles of Isaac Hunter's plantation. In 1792 the commissioners appointed by the General Assembly selected Joel Lane's tract of 1,000 acres, described in the deed of sale as "beginning at four sassafrasses, two white oaks, two persimmons, and one elm ....," and purchased it for f 1,378 (roughly equivalent to $2,756). With William Christmas as surveyor they completed the plan of Raleigh within five days, plotting a city of 400 acres from the 1,000-acre tract. They set aside, in addition to five public squares, 256 building lots of one acre each, geometrically separated by wide streets. The commissioners then named the streets and squares and began to sell off the lots, the proceeds going into a fund to build a statehouse on Union Square.

Nestled in a fine oak forest at the time of its founding almost 200 years ago, Raleigh, capital of North Carolina, is known today as the City of Oaks.

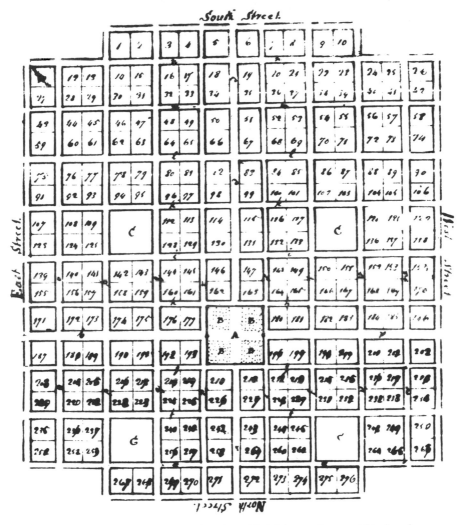

With William Christmas as surveyor, this plan of Raleigh was drawn within five days after the state purchased land for a capital.

north

The Capitol

★ **Begin at the Capitol**
1 **North Carolina Museum of Natural History**
2 **Legislative Building**
3 **Archives and History/ State Library Building**
4 **Executive Mansion***
5 **Lewis-Smith House***
6 **Andrews-Duncan House***
7 **Hawkins-Hartness House***
8 **Heck-Andrews House***
9 **Capehart House***
10 **Seaboard Coastline Office Building***

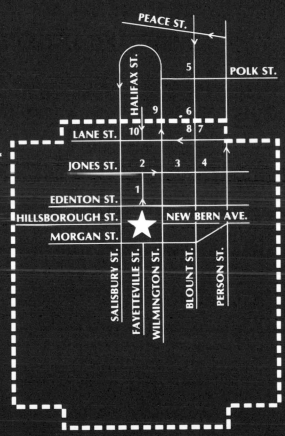

*Listed on the National Register of Historic Places and designated a Raleigh Historic Site.

The Capitol's "peanut man," Jess Broyles

North Carolina's Capitol is noted for the purity of its Greek Revival design.

North Carolina's Capitols

The first statehouse, financed by the sale of Raleigh's original lots, was completed and occupied in 1794. It served not only as the center of state government but also as a community center. Lectures and balls were held there as well as performances by sleight-of-hand artists and dramatic companies. The spacious chambers of the statehouse were used for religious services, there being no organized churches or church buildings in the earliest years. On June 21, 1831, the statehouse caught fire from a solder pot left in the loft by a careless workman while he went to dinner. Some state papers were saved, but the building was destroyed.

When the General Assembly met in 1831 and again in 1832 to consider replacing the statehouse, Raleigh barely managed to remain the "unalterable capital of North Carolina." With no sustaining industry, no waterway, and no railroad, the city depended for its very existence on state government. When the issue finally was decided, the legislature appropriated $50,000 and employed New York architects Ithiel Towne and A. J. Davis. The supervising architect David Paton of Edinburgh recruited skilled masons from the North to shape the locally quarried stone.

A mule-drawn railroad, the first in North Carolina, hauled the blocks of granite from the quarry 1¼ miles southeast of the building site. A passenger car was added on Sundays "for the accommodation of such ladies and gentlemen as desired to take the exercise of a railroad airing."

When the site had been cleared and the foundation laid, the original $50,000 had been expended. During the seven years the Capitol was under construction, the legislature made five more appropriations for the building — a total cost of $531,000, three times the annual revenue of the state. The cornerstone was laid on July 4, 1833, by Governor David L. Swain and the building was completed in 1840.

Museum of Natural History

Department of Agriculture Annex
101 Halifax Street
Hours: 9:00 AM - 5:00 PM Monday through Saturday
*   2:00 PM - 5:00 PM Sunday*
Admission: Free
Information: 829-7450

George, the 14-foot-long, 108-pound Indian python, has long been the star performer at the Museum of Natural History, although George does nothing but eat once every six months. Even when the curator takes George for a walk, nothing exciting happens— fortunately.

George is only one of many exhibits: the museum's three floors, undergoing renovation but still open to the public, contain collections relating to animal, plant, and geological resources of North Carolina. In addition to the four rare whale skeletons, exhibits include minerals, shells, fossils, and early Indian artifacts. The recently-renovated bird hall exhibits birds native to the state, including owls, hawks, and hummingbirds. The museum's live snake collection contains all varieties of poisonous snakes found in North Carolina.

The Museum of Natural History, maintained by the North Carolina Department of Agriculture and visited by over 200,000 people a year, is one of the state's most popular museums. In addition to preparing and maintaining exhibits, the museum has an education program that includes slides, film strips, and traveling exhibits.

Legislative Building

Jones Street
Hours: 8:30 AM - 5:30 PM Monday through Saturday
*   2:00 PM - 5:00 PM Sunday*
Information: 829-7928

The State Legislative Building, first occupied by the 1963 General Assembly, is unusual in that it is devoted solely to the legislative branch of state government. Designed by Edward Durell Stone in association with Holloway-Reeves, Architects, the three-story building is classical in character, reflecting both Western and Eastern cultures.

How to Get Out of the Legislative Building

Visitors to the North Carolina Legislative Building always have one thing in common: they are lost.

And they're not the only ones. On any given day, a goodly portion of the people working there are lost too.

Some conceal their predicament better than others. They pretend to look at the elegant interior, the graceful corridors, the sparkling pools with the fresh green plants draping overhead. They stare at the rows of little offices lining the corridors and glance upward at the second story balcony. But if one looks closely, one can see their eyes flickering nervously as they walk around and around and around. After circling four identical courtyards a number of times, people tend to exhibit symptoms of being trapped in a maze. They cling to the hope that if they just keep walking long enough, they will find where they are going.

This, however, is not necessarily the case. For since the spacious and lovely courtyards look alike to even the most practiced observer, one can walk around the same courtyards without realizing it.

Some visitors to the legislature become so hopelessly confused that they become desperate. One young man was stalled on the second floor one evening when the building was practically empty. He walked into a representative's office and asked the secretary forlornly, "Once you get into this place, is there any way to get out? Or do you have to stay forever?"

Motioning for the secretary to come look over the balcony into the first floor courtyard below, he said, "I think I've figured out what to do. If I leap over this railing and jump into the hanging flower pot, grab a sliding vine and land in the pool, I can get downstairs."

There are other ways to get out of the building. One legislative aide advises visitors to bring a bag of popcorn and leave a trail. Some prefer to be more scientific. So there is a numerical method for finding your way around. The following technique has been known to work for the few people who are able to remember it.

The building is divided into four quadrants, with four nearly identical courtyards.

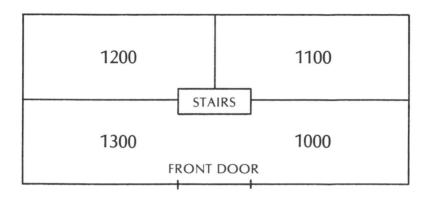

If the numbers on the door are in the 1100 range you know you are in the upper right corner of the building and must walk back through the 1000s to get out the front door. If you are in the 1200s, you can go around the 1300s to the front door. Those desiring any other entrance or exit will have to stumble around for themselves.

Unfortunately, the above scheme is not foolproof even for those who have worked in the building for a long time. Once when a veteran television producer was guiding a group of people through the building, he began to boast how well he knew his way around it. He had been working at the legislature for years, he told them, so getting around was easy.

With that, he walked the group to an exit, opened the door, and led them into a broom closet.

Linda Grimsley

Linda Grimsley, author of *Gorilla in the Kitchen*, teaches the Writers' Workshop at North Carolina State University with Sam Ragan.

North Carolina Museum of History

Archives and History/State Library Building*
109 East Jones Street
Hours: 8:30 AM - 5:30 PM Monday through Saturday
*   2:00 PM - 5:00 PM Sunday*
Admission: Free
Information: 829-3894

From "Stone Age to Space Age," the Museum of History depicts North Carolina's past. The first floor provides a social, economic, and political history of the state. Junior Historian award-winning projects and the Cutten Silver Collection are exhibited on the first floor where a sales desk is also maintained. The mezzanine features life-styles — how North Carolinians lived, dressed, and traveled. The second floor contains special exhibitions. Docents demonstrate weaving, spinning, and pottery-making. On week-days guided tours and artifact "Touch Talks" are available if a request is received one week in advance.

On Sunday afternoons at 3:00 PM the museum sponsors "Month of Sundays," free family-interest programs such as concerts, lectures, demonstrations, and movies in the Archives and History Auditorium. Through education and extension services, which include a Mobile Museum of History, slide programs, and the Tar Heel Junior Historian Association, the museum reaches and benefits North Carolinians throughout the state.

*A ramp at the Blount Street entrance is available for physically handicapped visitors.

North Carolina State Archives

Archives and History/State Library Building*
109 East Jones Street
Hours: 8:00 AM - 5:30 PM Monday through Friday
*   8:30 AM - 5:30 PM Saturday*
Information: 829-3952

The North Carolina archives contains the documentary heritage of the state. Available to the citizens of the state for research purposes, holdings include virtually all permanently valuable county records from the colonial period to about 1910, records of state agencies since about 1776, and private papers of persons important to the history of the state. In addition, there are materials copied from both English and Spanish archives relating to the colonial period, and there is a large military collection which contains material from the French and Indian War through World War II. Administered by the Archives and Records Section, Division of Archives and History, the archives is open to the public upon registration and suitable identification.

North Carolina State Library

Archives and History/State Library Building*
109 East Jones Street
Hours: 8:00 AM - 5:30 PM Monday through Friday
*   8:30 AM - 5:30 PM Saturday (for genealogical services)*
Information: 829-3270

Through the Information Network services offered by the North Carolina State Library, the resources of libraries throughout the state are made available to every citizen. Any librarian can forward a request by a toll-free WATS line to the State Library. Books and other materials can be sent to local libraries via interlibrary loan and photocopy services. The State Library is a division of the Department of Cultural Resources.

*A ramp at the Blount Street entrance is available for physically handicapped visitors.

Executive Mansion

200 North Blount Street
Open to the Public at Regularly Scheduled Hours
Information: 829-3456

An outstanding example of Victorian architecture in the restrained Queen Anne style, the Executive Mansion was designed by Samuel Sloan of Philadelphia and his assistant, Adolphus Gustavus Bauer. It was built over a period of nine years by prisoners and skilled craftsmen. Native materials were used wherever possible: the brownstone for the wall trim came from quarries in

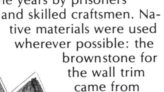

Anson County; the brick was handmade from Wake County clay by prisoners, some of the bricks still bearing the initials or names of the men who made them. The interior finish is North Carolina wood and the front steps, which replaced the original ones of Cherokee marble, are North Carolina granite. Since Governor Daniel G. Fowle moved into the newly-completed Executive Mansion in 1891, it has undergone two major renovations. The mansion has obtained many of its present furnishings and objects of art through the efforts of the Executive Mansion Fine Arts Committee.

The Ghost of Governor Fowle

In 1891, Daniel G. Fowle became the first North Carolina governor to occupy the new Executive Mansion that had replaced—after long delay—the Governor's Palace erected in 1816 at the south end of Fayetteville Street. The cost of the mansion had been greater than anticipated, and the allowance for furnishings was quite limited. In fact, Governor Fowle moved his own furniture into the official residence. Additionally, he ordered for himself an oversized bed of figured mahogany, heavy and fashionable. Tradition says that the governor, a widower, slept in the large bed with his young son. Governor Fowle died before his term was completed, some say in this very bed. In any case, the bed was to remain in use through the passing years, a mute witness of change, until the term of Governor Robert W. Scott.

A tall man, Governor Scott found the bed too short for his comfort. After a conference with Mrs. Scott, he determined to purchase a more comfortable, modern bed. Governor Fowle's was relegated to storage space on the third floor of the Executive Mansion.

Not long after its replacement, Governor and Mrs. Scott were sitting in the Fowle bedroom about 10:00 P.M. Suddenly from within the wall where the head of the old bed had stood there came a distinct knock, followed by subsequent knocks in gradually increasing tempo, lasting about a minute. Because the knocking recurred about the same time every night afterwards, a search for its origin was instigated. In spite of a thorough investigation, no physical cause for the sound could be determined.

At the time, Governor Scott said of the mysterious noise, "We, of course, do not believe in ghosts. However, the knocking does occur, and it is usually about the same time each night. For lack of a better explanation, we have named the knock the Governor Fowle Ghost. We assume that it is the ghost of Governor Fowle, requesting that the bed in which he died be replaced in the room."

Today the bed is no longer in the mansion. It is stored in the Division of Archives and History with other artifacts of North Carolina's past. If Governor Fowle is still looking for his bed, he will have to travel from the grand Victorian house on Blount Street to a gleaming, starkly modern, white building nearby.

Leonidas Betts

Leonidas Betts is editor of the *North Carolina Folklore Journal*

The Lewis-Smith house was moved from its original site to make way for the State Government Mall.

Lewis-Smith House

515 North Blount Street
Private Residence — Not Open to the Public

Moved from its original site at 515 North Wilmington Street, the Lewis-Smith house was the home of Charles Lee Smith, one of North Carolina's most distinguished and respected men in the fields of education and publishing. The house is one of the few early Greek Revival buildings surviving in Raleigh. Built about 1855 for Dr. Augustus M. Lewis, a member of the General Assembly, the house has been purchased by the state for eventual adaptive use.

Andrews-Duncan House

407 North Blount Street

This fine Victorian house, designed by G. S. Appleget and built in 1873 for Colonel A. B. Andrews, is now owned by the state and used for offices. The ancient white oak known as the "Henry Clay Oak" stands in the yard on the North Street side. It was under this tree in 1844, when the William Polk house stood here, that Henry Clay, popular Whig candidate for president of the United States, is said to have written his famous letter on the Texas question. The letter, published in *The National Intelligencer*, was thought to have cost Clay the presidency.

Heck-Andrews House

309 North Blount Street
Private Residence — Not Open to the Public

Built in 1869-1870 for Colonel Jonathan M. Heck, this house may be said to have set the tone for Blount Street. It is a superb example of the flamboyant Second Empire style popular throughout the country at that time. The most striking features of the house are its high mansard roof, repetitive detail, and fanciful tower. Specifications for the house, hand-written by its architect, G. S. Appleget, are on file in the state archives.

Hawkins-Hartness House

310 North Blount Street

Noted for the unusually restrained exterior design for its period and for the fine craftsmanship of its interiors, the Hawkins-Hartness house was built after 1884, a few years before the Executive Mansion. Dr. Hawkins had a 6,000-gallon cistern in the north garden to supply filtered drinking water for his household and for the Executive Mansion across the street. He would invite each new governor to have water from the cistern, and "Uncle David," who worked at the mansion for many years, would come with his cedar bucket and tote the water over to the mansion. The Hawkins-Hartness house is owned by the state and used for offices.

Capehart House

403 North Wilmington Street

With the exception of the Executive Mansion, this house is Raleigh's finest example of the Queen Anne style of architecture popular in the late 19th and early 20th centuries. Its turrets and towers, turned woodwork, and stained glass windows are typical of this style. Built about 1898 for Lucy Moore Capehart, daughter of noted Attorney General B. F. Moore, the house is now owned by the state and has been used for offices since 1971. Its future is uncertain in view of the proposed State Government Mall.

The Hawkins-Hartness house was once a fashionable and formal Victorian home.

At Home on Blount Street

Once Raleigh's most fashionable residential avenue, North Blount Street was the scene of formal living and lavish entertaining in the late 1800s and early 1900s. Mrs. Mattie Bailey Haywood, who spent her childhood with her great-uncle and great-aunt, Dr. and Mrs. A. B. Hawkins, at 310 North Blount Street (the Hawkins-Hartness house) recalled that at least five well-trained servants kept the household running smoothly. There were a maid, a cook, a butler, and a yard man, in addition to one or two women who did the laundry in soapstone tubs in the basement. Twice a week the yard man got down on his knees and cleaned the porch, 92 feet around.

Breakfast, served by the butler at eight o'clock, was a tremendous meal of broiled chicken, egg bread, and fish roe. The family sat down to dinner, another heavy meal, at two o'clock.

BLOUNT STREET IS FADING AWAY

When the children came home from school, they ate the hot dinner saved for them and then were free to play in the big yard, which was surrounded by a picket fence. In a corner of the yard were a tennis court, croquet grounds, and swings. Families on the street owned big victorias, and Mrs. Haywood recalled her uncle's pair of black horses, the netting on top of their heads making their ears stand up straight and giving them a "festive, circus-like appearance."

Dr. and Mrs. Hawkins' 50th wedding anniversary party in 1908 was a special occasion at 310 North Blount Street. "My aunt sent to Washington, D. C. for boxes of beautiful yellow daffodils and jonquils, yellow tulips and chrysanthemums, everything yellow," Mrs. Haywood said. "They ordered frozen molded desserts, and when the word was passed up the street that they were having their 50th wedding anniversary, the neighbors all stopped in. We had callers all day long."

ONE WAY

Seaboard Coast Line Railroad Office Building

325 Halifax Street

The arcaded cast-iron porches and shallow hip roof of the Italianate Seaboard Building are echoed by its nearest neighbor the Legislative Building. Constructed about 1861 with later additions, the Seaboard Building has been utilized for railroad administration for over 100 years. The state has purchased the building and plans to move it to make way for the mall.

The Seaboard Office Building is one of the oldest railroad buildings in the Southeast.

The Triumph of the Tornado

"The bells rang, the artillery roared, and the people cheered," reported the Raleigh Register, March 24, 1840, when "the first steam locomotive [the Tornado] that ever snorted amongst the hills of Crabtree reached the limits of our city and was enthusiastically welcomed with every demonstration of joy."

Before the railroad, both travelers and mail came and left by horseback, carriage, or stage. In the early 1800s, the stage arrived three evenings each week, stopping in front of either Casso's Inn or the Eagle Tavern, both of which faced the statehouse square. Citizens eagerly awaited the packets of letters and papers as well as news brought by travelers. According to the late historian W. G. Briggs, Andrew Jackson's victory over the British at New Orleans on January 8, 1815, was not known in Raleigh until the 17th of February — 40 days after the battle.

"In 1806," Mr. Briggs wrote, "the traveler left Petersburg [by stage] at the unearthly hour of three o'clock Wednesday morning, reached Warrenton in time for a late supper and lodged at the Inn; at four o'clock Thursday morning he resumed his seat in the uncomfortable coach, and if the horses made the schedule time and there were no mishaps, he alighted at Casso's Inn at six o'clock that afternoon."

When the 86-mile-long Raleigh and Gaston Railroad was completed, a traveler could reach Raleigh from Petersburg by train in 12 hours. The Raleigh and Gaston's first locomotive into Raleigh, the Tornado, is said to have pulled 30 loaded cars, or about 162 tons.

The Capitol ▶ east

★ The Capitol*
2 North Carolina Museum of Art
3 White-Holman House*
4 Haywood Hall*
5 State Bank*
6 Christ Church*
7 Richard B. Haywood House*
8 First Baptist Church
9 City Cemetery

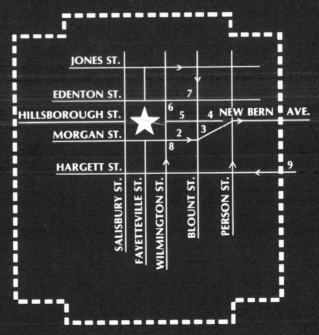

*Listed on the National Register of Historic Places and designated a Raleigh Historic Site.

North Carolina's Capitol

The Capitol — A Masterpiece

A superb example of Greek Revival architecture and now a National Historic Landmark, the Capitol was once called "a Grecian temple set on a hog pasture." An 1840 visitor wrote, "To see the Capitol of North Carolina is worth a walk on foot from Petersburg to Raleigh in the depth of winter, and on corduroy roads." The central rotunda of the cross-shaped building has a copper dome 97½ feet high. Exterior walls are native granite; interior, stone and brick. Today's visitor still walks on some of the original stone floors. There is no steel in the building; the original massive wooden truss system supports the roof. Gas lights replaced candles in 1866 and electric lights were installed in 1891.

Until the Civil War, servants lived in the Capitol to lay the fires and attend the needs of state officials. Except for a gash in a door, the building withstood Raleigh's surrender to Union troops. The stone steps were chipped, it is said, by barrels of whiskey rolled down them by carpetbaggers after the war.

Originally, the Capitol housed all three branches of state government, but only the secretary of state retains his office here now. The legislative halls and the traditional office for the governor are maintained for ceremonial occasions.

The House and Senate chambers are still furnished with the original desks, made in Raleigh by William Thompson. Thomas Sully's copy of Gilbert Stuart's "Lansdowne" portrait of George Washington, saved from the fire that destroyed the first statehouse, hangs in the Hall of the House.

Many years of heavy use have made some restoration necessary: the exterior has been steam cleaned and scrubbed and the original copper roof replaced with a new one. The cost of restoration, including the interior, will total nearly a million dollars — almost double the original cost of the building.

Canova's Washington

George Washington was "first in the hearts of the American people" when North Carolina decided to honor his memory with a statue. On the recommendation of Thomas Jefferson, the state commissioned "Old Canove" (Antonio Canova, 1757-1821) of Rome, Europe's most respected sculptor.

George Washington
by Antonio Canova.

In 1821 the marble statue of Washington in Roman toga, the Neoclassic fashion then in vogue, arrived in Raleigh. Spectators lined the roadside to watch "the father of our country" being pulled by oxen over the plank road from Fayetteville.

The statue was placed in the rotunda of the first statehouse where it was unveiled on December 24. According to Ben F. Williams, *North Carolina Museum of Art Bulletin*, 1957-58, "The statue, first significant sculpture to be imported, was considered everywhere in America the finest work of art in the country." When the statehouse burned in 1831, the people tried to save the statue; however, it was too heavy to move and the building's dome collapsed, crushing it.

In 1970 a second statue, pointed-up from the original model, was placed in the present Capitol where it stands in the rotunda.

North Carolina Museum of Art

107 East Morgan Street
Hours: 10:00 AM - 5:00 PM Tuesday through Saturday
2:00 PM - 6:00 PM Sunday
Closed Monday
Admission: Free
Information: 829-7568, weekdays; 829-3248, weekends

The North Carolina Artists Annual Exhibition is co-sponsored by North Carolina Museum of Art and North Carolina Art Society.

The North Carolina Museum of Art contains the finest collection of art in the Southeast. When the General Assembly appropriated $1,000,000 in 1947 "to purchase an art collection for the state," the museum acquired paintings by Homer, Rubens, Van Dyke, and Gainsborough. This appropriation attracted a gift from the Kress Foundation and the museum's Kress Collection of Renaissance and Baroque art is second in size only to that of the National Gallery of Art in Washington. Later acquisitions include Monet, Pisarro, Raphael, and Wyeth. The Mary Duke Biddle Gallery for the Blind, a pioneering effort, provides art to be explored through touch.

Staff and docents conduct tours of the permanent collection and special exhibitions. The museum holds Sunday afternoon lectures and concerts, creativity workshops for children, seminars for teachers, and other special programs. The North Carolina Art Society's Rental/Sales Gallery on the fourth floor exhibits and sells the works of contemporary artists. A bookstore is located on the first floor.

Founded and administered by the North Carolina State Art Society until 1961, the museum is now a section of the Department of Cultural Resources of North Carolina. The first state to use public funds on such a large scale for the purchase of art, North Carolina makes an annual appropriation to the museum's purchase fund.

Contemporary Art in Wake County

Contemporary art means the art of the present. To some the term may evoke images of the *avant-garde*, of elitism and mystery. These are romantic notions that get in the way of reality for art cannot survive without people. It can exist only where it finds stimulation, both complimentary and abrasive. A number of facts suggests that Wake County provides such stimulation.

First, there exists a significant group of skilled, enthusiastic amateurs. These people, who helped create the Pullen Park Arts and Crafts Center, open since 1961, now fill it with an average of 1,000 persons per month. Painting, drawing, weaving, ceramics, and pottery are staple offerings.

Second, there are a number of private galleries which are

flourishing because the collectors, the amateurs, and their friends help support them. This symbiosis is also instrumental in the success of the sidewalk shows and auctions which are regular features of Wake County life. Similarly, eager participation in the Raleigh Fine Arts Society exhibitions held in cooperation with the Wake County Public Libraries at the Olivia Raney Library is due to the sizable number of area artists as well as viewers.

In this context the professional artist can easily contribute knowledge and find stimulation and appreciation in return. For example, an extension course in painting offered by North Carolina State University for the past two decades is now legendary for its success. Out of those classes has grown a distinctive professional coterie of younger painters and printmakers who now exhibit and teach. Many School of Design faculty members, like their colleagues at other area colleges and universities, attract students who often remain in the area. In 1971, 25 of 180 exhibiting artists in the annual North Carolina Artists Exhibition at the North Carolina Museum of Art were from Raleigh or Wake County; in 1972, the numbers were 22 of 126. Vitality, however, always lies in looking at made things. Here one sees a delight in making that can be shared by viewer and artist alike. No false barriers separate "craft" from "art." The only barrier is that of a growing and expanding awareness which insists on separating *good* work from bad.

Charlotte V. Brown

Charlotte Vestal Brown is assistant associate professor of history of art and director of undergraduate studies for art history, Duke University.

White-Holman House

209 East Morgan Street
Private Residence — Not Open to the Public

William White, appointed secretary of state in 1798, was required by law to live in Raleigh and he began his house the same year. It was in this house in 1826 that Eleanor White married David L. Swain, later governor of the state and president of the University of North Carolina.

Because of the elaborate interior woodwork, it seems probable that the White-Holman house and Haywood Hall had the same builder. The house stayed in the White family until 1884 when William C. Holman purchased it. To save and restore the house, the city bought it in 1969 and placed it under the control of the Raleigh Historic Properties Commission. Future plans include turning the house to face New Bern Avenue and Haywood Hall.

Haywood Hall

211 New Bern Avenue
Private Residence — Not Open to the Public

Almost as old as the capital city itself, Haywood Hall is rich in North Carolina history. One of the finest Federal houses in Raleigh, it was built about 1799 by John Haywood, treasurer of North Carolina for 40 years, and has always been occupied by his family and descendants. The house stands on its original foundations of

locally quarried stone. Typical of the era, all its timbers were hand-hewn and held together by pegs or hand-wrought nails. The original furnishings, some of which still remain, were brought by ship from England to Charleston and on to Raleigh by mule.

Haywood Hall was the scene of assemblies and balls, and John Haywood entertained every member of each General Assembly. "This is the only Day our house has been still for weeks," Mrs. Haywood wrote her mother on December 20, 1803. "Sunday .... Mr. H. invited 30 Gentlemen to Dinner, Six and Twenty at the Long Table and four at a side Table — and that has been the Number every other Day since. ..." Writing that she had "people all day and the children all night," in addition to staying up until twelve and one o'clock to prepare for guests, Eliza Haywood concluded, "I am almost worn out and Broke Down with Fatigue and want of rest ...."

(Quotation from letter of Eliza Haywood, December 20, 1803, in Ernest Haywood Collection, Southern Historical Collection, University of North Carolina Library, Chapel Hill.)

State Bank of North Carolina (NCNB)

11 New Bern Avenue

During the War of 1812, when it was feared the British would attack the North Carolina coast, all specie money was moved inland and the State Bank built this structure, completed in 1814. Called "two porches with a house between," the State Bank's novel architectural style is essentially Federal. The exterior is handmade brick with columns also made of brick, stuccoed over with coarse sand and mortar. The interior retains some of the original mantels and doors, and the suspended circular stairway is original. Colonel William Polk, Revolutionary War hero and first president of the bank, made his home in the building.

After the Civil War Christ Church bought the structure for $9,925, using it until 1968 when it was slated for demolition. To save the building, the North Carolina National Bank purchased and renovated it, moving it 100 feet southeast of its original site. The building is currently serving as headquarters for the North Carolina Bicentennial.

The State Bank has been called "two porches with a house between."

Richard B. Haywood House

127 East Edenton Street
Private Residence — Not Open to the Public

One of Raleigh's fine examples of Greek Revival architecture, the Richard B. Haywood house was completed in 1854 on land that has been in the family since 1799. Dr. Haywood is said to have been his own architect, and it is thought that Mrs. Haywood insisted on the beautifully executed bay windows. The beauty of the house,

which has always been occupied by Dr. Haywood's family and lineal descendants, lies in the sophisticated use of proportion and line rather than elaborate decoration. The house contains many of its original furnishings, including a pair of tall pier glasses set on consoles with marble tops and foliated feet which were specially ordered for the parlor.

Richard B. Haywood's friendship with Major General Francis P. Blair, commander of the Union's occupation forces in Raleigh, helped to secure the peaceful occupation of the city. Both men had been students at the University of North Carolina, and General Blair selected Dr. Haywood's home for his headquarters. On the night the Union troops received news of President Lincoln's assassination, General Blair threw a blue Federal uniform on Dr. Haywood's bed, saying, "Dick, you're a Confederate surgeon, but tonight it may be necessary for you to turn yourself into a Yankee general." Fortunately, Blair's fears were not realized. When Generals Grant and Sherman visited Raleigh, they were entertained by General Blair at the Haywood home.

First Baptist Church

101 South Wilmington Street

The First Baptist Church was founded in 1812 with 23 members—nine of them white and fourteen, black — and for 56 years the membership remained bi-racial. In 1868 the black members withdrew and formed a separate congregation, occupying a building in the 400-block of North Salisbury Street for 36 years. The Reverend William Warwick was the first pastor of this church after the separation. The cornerstone of the present building was laid in 1904.

Christ Episcopal Church

120 East Edenton Street

Christ Episcopal Church was established in 1821. Its first rector, John S. Ravenscroft, was first Bishop of North Carolina. The present building, designed by Richard Upjohn, architect of Trinity Church in New York City and founder of the American Institute of Architects, was completed in 1853 and consecrated in 1854. Built of locally quarried stone, Christ Church, with its superb hammer-beam roof, is an important example of Upjohn's Early Gothic Revival style. The bell tower was completed in 1861 and the gilded weathercock was set in place by a little boy.

The 1921 parish house and chapel were skillfully designed by Upjohn's grandson, Hobart Upjohn, to blend with the older structure. The present parish house addition was erected in 1970.

City Cemetery

South East and Hargett Streets

City Cemetery was established in 1798 when the General Assembly authorized Raleigh to set aside land for use as a burying ground; there is, however, some indication that the land was used for burying purposes prior to that date. The cemetery was divided into four quarters, with the northern half used for the burial of Raleigh citizens; the southwest quarter, for visitors; and the southeast quarter, for blacks. Buried in City Cemetery are Jacob Johnson, father of President Andrew Johnson; John Rex, donor of Rex Hospital; Joseph Gales, publisher of the *Raleigh Register;* Governor Charles Manly; and many other well-known figures. The cemetery's iron fence enclosed the Capitol grounds from 1847 to 1898.

Christ Episcopal Church, built of native stone, was consecrated in 1854.

west ◀ **The Capitol**
▼
south

★ **Begin at the Capitol**   **5 Dodd-Hinsdale House***
1 Briggs Hardware*   **6 Raleigh Water Tower***
2 Federal Building*   **7 First Presbyterian Church**
3 Memorial Auditorium   **8 Joel Lane House, Wakefield***
4 First Baptist Church   **9 Elmwood**

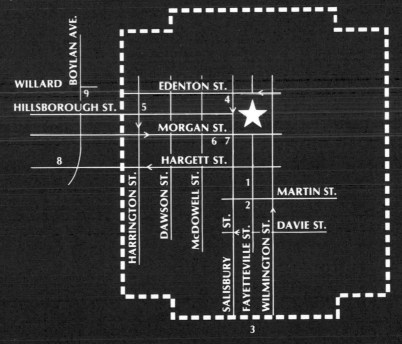

*Listed on the National Register of Historic Places and designated a Raleigh Historic Site.

Fayetteville Street Mall

From Union Square to Civic Center

When the state bought its 1,000 acres from Joel Lane, the portion of land west of Capitol Square and Salisbury Street had been cleared; but the rest, including the site of the Capitol, was virgin forest. A large sassafras tree near the southwest corner marked a deer stand where a relative of Joel Lane is said to have shot 40 deer.

Through the years Union Square has undergone many changes. In 1857 thousands of people came to the dedication of the first statue to be placed on the square, the statue of George Washington, a bronze replica of Jean Antoine Houdon's marble original in the Capitol at Richmond. In 1875, according to the late historian Fred A. Olds, "in the northwest corner was the wood-house, the house of public comfort and the state bell (in a belfry 25 feet high) which rang to announce the sittings of the supreme court and occasionally meetings of the legislature. In the southwest corner was the state arsenal, a small two-story affair, of brick." An iron fence with four gates surrounded the Capitol grounds.

As Union Square, now called Capitol Square, has changed, so have the streets around it. Fayetteville Street, one of Raleigh's first principal thoroughfares, has marked Raleigh's history while continuing to meet the demands of progress. In 1808 a future president, Andrew Johnson, was born in a house near the present site of the Ambassador Theater. Fayetteville Street's old Yarborough House (1852-1928), a hotel maintained "on the highest plane" and world renowned, hosted such prominent Americans as Helen Keller, William Jennings Bryan, and Presidents Theodore Roosevelt, William Howard Taft, and Woodrow Wilson, and served from 1871-1891 as the unofficial residence of several of North Carolina's governors.

The Federal Building (1878) and Briggs Hardware (1874) have survived to witness the greatest change for this old street as it becomes a mall extending from the Capitol to the Civic Center just north of Memorial Auditorium. The Civic Center, with an area of 170,000 square feet, is designed with facilities for conventions, trade shows, and sports events, with meeting rooms for groups of all sizes. The 1932 Memorial Auditorium at the foot of Fayetteville Street is the center for the performing arts and part of the Civic Center Complex.

North Carolina Symphony

Memorial Auditorium
Information: 829-2750

The North Carolina Symphony plays eight concerts during the season at Memorial Auditorium, its first permanent home. Programs are varied and feature guest artists. Although admission is by season membership, tickets to individual concerts are sold at the door after

p.turner '75

8:00 PM on the night of the concert if seats are available. Visitors are permitted to sit in on rehearsals at Memorial Auditorium if they contact the symphony office first.

The North Carolina Symphony is composed of 70 musicians, with two Little Symphonies of 35 musicians each, a brass quintet, a string quartet, and a woodwind quintet. Begun in 1932 and reorganized in 1939 by Dr. Benjamin F. Swalin, Conductor Emeritus, the symphony performs nearly 225 concerts a season in North Carolina and Virginia, traveling over 18,000 miles. Its education program includes children's concerts, a "Discovery" series, and competitions for young musicians.

The symphony is a section of the North Carolina Department of Cultural Resources. Its parent organization, the North Carolina Symphony Society, Inc., contributes active support.

Briggs Hardware

220 Fayetteville Street

The Briggs building, home of one of Raleigh's oldest continuous businesses, was built in 1874 and remains essentially unchanged. The 19th century structure, four stories high in front, has a rich red brick facade with handsome details.

The business was opened on this site in 1865 by James Dodd and Thomas Briggs, who is said to have safeguarded his fortune through Raleigh's surrender by hiding his gold and silver in lead pipes near the edge of the city. Soon after the present building was completed, Dodd retired and Briggs formed a partnership with his two sons. The 1875-76 Raleigh City Directory lists the firm, Thomas H. Briggs & Sons, Inc. as "purveyors of Hardware, Cutlery, House Furnishing Goods, Wagon and Buggy Material," among other items.

Over the years other uses were made of the upper floors of the Briggs building which housed, at various times, a barber shop, the YMCA, a Catholic Church congregation, the Raleigh Little Theater, and a number of attorneys and insurance companies.

Services were first held in the First Baptist Church in 1859.

In 1972 when the business was 107 years old, James E. Briggs ran an advertisement in the paper that concluded, "We want to stay around at least another 107 years if it's only to see 'what the heck will happen next'."

Federal Building — Century Postal Station

300 Fayetteville Street

Raleigh's first federally constructed post office was built in Reconstruction days, 1874-1878. The design of this building is typical of that used by the federal government throughout the country in the late 19th century. The old Federal Building and the contemporary courthouse next to it present a dramatic picture of Raleigh's changing urban scene.

First Baptist Church

Corner Salisbury and Edenton Streets

Organized in 1812, this is the second oldest congregation in Raleigh and the second oldest church building. First occupied in 1859, this Neo-Gothic building designed by a British architect, William Percival, retains much of its original appearance. During the Civil War, the church bell was donated to the Confederacy to be melted down for cannon, and the basement was used by local women to make uniforms, towels, haversacks, and mattresses. Soon after the war, the black members resigned to form their own congregation. The education building, designed by Haskins and Rice, Architects, and completed in 1970, is of contemporary design with Gothic influence. The church is designated a Raleigh Historic Site.

Betty Eichenberger

Dodd-Hinsdale House

330 Hillsborough Street
Private Residence — Not Open to the Public

"As a small child, I always ran by because to me it was the castle where the old witch kept Hansel and Gretel."
—Elizabeth Ashe Flint in a letter to Elizabeth Reid

This proud Victorian home was built about 1887, possibly by Thomas Briggs, for William H. Dodd, one-time Raleigh mayor. John Hinsdale bought the house in 1890 and his family and descendants occupied it until 1971. The most striking feature is the Second Empire tower, its three stages rising 1½ stories high. The tower is crowned with a mansard cupola.

First Presbyterian Church

112 South Salisbury Street

The First Presbyterian Church was organized in 1816 in the old statehouse, its first pastor being the Reverend William McPheeters, D. D. The congregation purchased a lot on the southwest corner of Salisbury and Morgan streets and erected a brick building, dedicated in 1818, which stood for nearly 80 years and was long the common meeting place of Protestants in Raleigh. Between 1831, when the old statehouse was destroyed by fire, and 1840, when the new Capitol was completed, the North Carolina Supreme Court met in the old Session House or Lecture Room which had been erected in 1825 beside the church. The 1835 Constitutional Convention held its sessions in the church, and Sherman's army used the building after the Civil War. The present Romanesque Revival structure built in 1900 is designated a Raleigh Historic Site.

Raleigh Water Tower/AIA Tower

115 West Morgan Street

Before Raleigh installed its 1887 waterworks, citizens had to depend on wells, springs, and cisterns. Even though Raleigh had bought its first fire engine in 1802, fire continued to be a common danger. After the post office burned in 1851, *The Standard* commented, "This fire has, we think, conclusively demonstrated two things to our citizens: first, the danger resulting from wooden buildings in a crowded part of town; and secondly, the great importance of water facilities and some efficient fire organization. .... But what could they [the citizens] do but fight the fire, as they did, with axes, beams of wood, ropes, and their naked hands?" A Raleigh woman, who is reported to have saved her home by soaking the roof with wet bed quilts, also saved a store by pouring 12 barrels of vinegar on it when the wells ran dry.

This water tower was built in 1887 of Wake County granite and hand-made brick. It consists of two buildings, the front one having an attached octagonal tower that rises 85 feet with walls three feet thick. The tower served the city until 1924 when it was abandoned and its 30-foot-high, 100,000-gallon iron tank was removed from the top.

The late William Henley Deitrick, architect, purchased the water tower in 1938 and renovated it for his offices. Originally, the interior of the tower, which had a dirt floor, had nothing to break its height. Nine great timber supports rose from the ground to the water tank, reached by a spiral stair. These timbers were removed by Mr. Deitrick who divided the tower into four levels. In 1963 "the structure was conveyed to the North Carolina Chapter of the American Institute of Architects to be used as their state headquarters with the assurance .... that the property should be held as a historic site without substantial change ...." The water tower is an excellent example of imaginative adaptive use of a building slated for destruction.

Joel Lane House (Wakefield)

728 West Hargett Street

Once the largest and most important house for miles around, Joel Lane's home "Wakefield," built before 1770, was the birthplace of the city of Raleigh. It was here in 1792 that the commissioners appointed to select a site for the capital met. After inspecting all the land offered for purchase, they selected a 1,000-acre tract owned by Lane and adjacent to Wakefield.

As a member of the General Assembly of 1770-1771, Lane introduced the bill that created Wake County. He later represented the new county at the Provincial Congress in 1775 and 1776. For 11 of the 14 sessions between 1782 and 1795, he was a state senator. Because of Lane's prominence and hospitality and the convenience of his home at the crossing of two main highways, Wakefield was a popular stopping place. Lane built a separate ordinary, or tavern, to accommodate travelers, both friends and strangers. The General Assembly met there during the Revolutionary War in 1781 when Thomas Burke was elected governor.

Wakefield, a good example of North Carolina Colonial architecture with a gambrel roof typical of the 18th century, originally stood 100 yards from its present location and faced east, overlooking the site of the planned capital. When restoration is completed, Wakefield will be furnished with 18th century furniture and accessories and will be open to the public at regularly scheduled hours. A gift shop will be available. The Raleigh Garden Club is assisting with the planting of a period garden. Wakefield is owned by the National Society of Colonial Dames of America in the State of North Carolina and leased to Joel Lane House, Inc. for restoration, operation, and maintenance.

Elmwood

16 North Boylan Avenue
Private Residence — Not Open to the Public

This Federal townhouse, built about 1815, has a side-hall plan and fine Adam interiors. John Louis Taylor, first chief justice of the North Carolina Supreme Court, bought 100 acres for $300 from John Haywood in 1813 and on this land built the house which was later owned by William Gaston, also a justice of the supreme court and author of the state song. Another prominent owner was Samuel Ashe, Confederate captain, newspaper editor, and North Carolina historian.

Early Neighborhoods

★ **Begin at the Capitol**
1 **Mordecai Historic Park**
2 **Historic Oakwood***
3 **Oakwood Cemetery***
4 **Oberlin — Reconstruction Era Village**

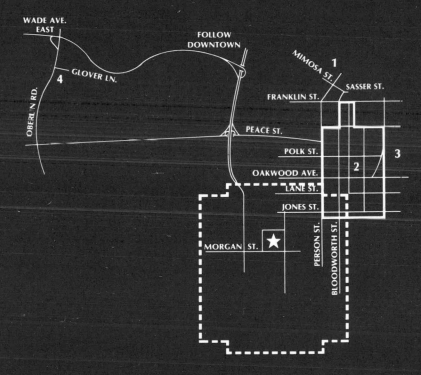

*Listed on the National Register of Historic Places and designated a Raleigh Historic Site.

Andrew Johnson birthplace and Ellen Mordecai garden

Mordecai Historic Park

1 Mimosa Street
Hours: October - May   10:00 AM - 1:00 PM Tuesday through Thursday
                                  2:00 PM - 4:00 PM Sunday
June - September   2:00 PM - 4:00 PM Sunday
Information: 834-4844

Mordecai House was built about 1785, with the Greek Revival portico added in 1826.

Part of the huge antebellum Mordecai plantation, this city block with the Mordecai House and two original dependencies was purchased in 1967 by the city of Raleigh and is now supervised and developed as a historic park by the Raleigh Historic Properties Commission. Other buildings that have been moved to the park include the 1842 Allen Kitchen, the Badger-Iredell Law Office, the Andrew Johnson birthplace, and another early office building thought to have been used for several antebellum years as Raleigh's post office.

The main house and kitchen are open to the public at regularly scheduled times and as each additional building is restored, it will be open also. Information about lectures, demonstrations, and other activities at Mordecai Historic Park can be obtained by calling 834-4844 or by writing P. O. Box 0, Raleigh, N. C. 27611.

Mordecai House

The Mordecai House holds the changing history of a family and a community. Joel Lane, who owned the land, is thought to have built this house for his son Henry about 1785, several years before Lane sold land to the state for its capital. The house became known as the Mordecai House after Moses Mordecai married into the Lane family.

The original 18th century house was a simple hall-and-parlor frame dwelling with an east-west orientation. After the death of Moses Mordecai, his widow employed the architect William Nichols to enlarge the original structure. Five rooms facing south and the impressive portico were added, changing the house into an early Greek Revival mansion. Nichols was the architect who had remodeled the old statehouse in 1820-1822, and this 1826 addition to the Mordecai House is significant as an existing example of his work. Many of the family's original furnishings, which range from 18th century to early 20th, including furniture, portraits, books, and decorative pieces, reflect the lives of those who lived here. The Mordecai House is listed on the National Register of Historic Places and designated a Raleigh Historic Site.

Allen Kitchen

Built in 1842 and originally located in Anson County, this kitchen was given to the North Carolina Division of Archives and History by the three sons of Mrs. Mary Allen Huntley. Located on the approximate site of the Mordecai kitchen, it is furnished with utensils of the period.

Ellen Mordecai Garden

Just behind the kitchen, a garden has been re-created according to the reminiscences of Ellen Mordecai in *Gleanings from Long Ago*. Ellen was born in the Mordecai House in 1820 and played in the garden as a child. Many of the plants are mentioned by Ellen in her book; but all plants in the garden — flowers, shrubs, vegetables, and herbs — are plants that were available in the 1830s, such as bee balm, baby's breath, lavender, and lilacs. In one corner is the little "wheelbarrow house" described in the book, and an orchard of peaches and apples adjoins a scuppernong arbor.

Andrew Johnson Birthplace

Mordecai Historic Park is the fifth location for the little house in which Andrew Johnson, 17th president of the United States, was born. The house was purchased in 1904 by the Wake County Committee of the North Carolina Society of Colonial Dames of America and presented to the city of Raleigh. Unfortunately, its furnishings of the period, in storage for the last move, were burned. The house will be refurnished through donations and purchases.

The house originally stood on Fayetteville Street near Casso's Inn where Andrew's father Jacob Johnson was hostler. In 1812 when Andrew was three years old, his father died from over-exertion caused by saving a friend from drowning. Andrew left Raleigh at the age of 16 and eventually settled in Greeneville, Tennessee.

The Andrew Johnson birthplace is being restored by the city through the Raleigh Historic Properties Commission. When it is restored and refurnished, it will be open to the public at regularly scheduled times.

The Andrew Johnson house was moved from Pullen Park in two sections to avoid power lines.

Badger-Iredell Law Office

Built about 1810, this office once stood on the northwest corner of North Dawson and Edenton streets. It served as law office for George Edmund Badger, lawyer, legislator, judge, United States senator, and secretary of the navy. James Iredell, Jr., governor of North Carolina, 1827-1828, also used this building as a law office. It is being restored by the Wake County Bar Association as an early 19th century law office.

Historic Oakwood

Oakwood, Raleigh's oldest existing neighborhood and first historic district, is listed on the National Register of Historic Places. The great variety of architectural styles found in Oakwood reflects the tastes of the Victorian South and the skill of local architects and builders. The records of Thomas H. Briggs & Sons indicate that firm's involvement in the construction of a large number of the houses.

Queen Anne, Second Empire, Neoclassical Revival, Gothic Revival, and Eastlake styles of architecture were adapted to the North Carolina climate by such features as French doors and floor-length windows, spacious piazzas and latticed rear-service porches. There are turrets, gables, cupolas, mansard roofs, stained glass windows, bay windows, and even a mansard tower with a balcony.

After World War I, when the widespread use of the automobile led to the development of Raleigh suburbs, Oakwood seemed destined to decay into an area of boarding houses and apartments. Although the houses deteriorated, the Depression kept them from being changed. By 1970 Oakwood had begun to attract young professionals. Residents formed the Society for the Preservation of Historic Oakwood, and the rehabilitation of Oakwood began. By 1975 residents had restored 52 houses. Instead of leveling the existing homes for an expressway as planned, the city council named Oakwood a historic district, protected by a special commission.

The Upchurch-Stronach house, 414 North Bloodworth Street, is characterized by its eccentric but charming use of Queen Anne features such as twin turrets and a colored rosette window.

The Tucker House, built in the early 20th century on North Blount Street, was moved one block east to 414 Person Street where it will serve as a community center for residents of the Oakwood and Mordecai sections. It was given to the city of Raleigh by its owner, Garland S. Tucker, Jr.

The style of this house, 503 East Jones Street, has been called "Steamboat Gothic." It is one of three houses, all Second Empire in design, which were built speculatively for Jonathan M. Heck and closely resemble his own mansion at 309 North Blount Street.

Oakwood Cemetery

In 1866 Raleigh was ordered by the commanding Union general to remove the Confederate dead from graves near the Confederates' Pettigrew Hospital in order to provide space for the establishment of National Cemetery. Land was needed and Henry Mordecai gave 2¼ acres for the reburial of Confederate soldiers and sailors. The Ladies Memorial Association of Wake County had organized and its members now began "putting the cemetery in order." The following year they chose May 10, the anniversary of Andrew Jackson's death, to decorate the graves. The city was under martial law and no public observance of the day was allowed.

"Indeed, the threat was made that if the women went to the cemetery in a procession, they would be fired upon without further warning. So [they] gathered in groups of not more than two or three, each one bearing her crosses and wreaths, and wended their way to the cemetery, closely followed and watched by a Federal officer to see that no procession was formed.

"At this time there were no exercises of any kind, not even a prayer, and it demanded some courage and independence from those who walked under dripping skies through ankle-deep mud of the country road to fulfill this poor duty to our fallen heroes." This account was recorded by Mrs. Garland Jones, president of the Ladies Memorial Association in 1893. When the United Daughters of the Confederacy erected a House of Memory here in 1936, there were over 2800 graves of Confederate soldiers and sailors, reinterred from cemeteries all over the country.

The adjacent Oakwood Cemetery was established in 1870 on land bought from Mordecai by the Raleigh Cemetery Association. Many historically prominent North Carolinians, including Treasurer John Haywood, Chief Justice Richard M. Pearson, and Governors David L. Swain, Jonathan Worth, Daniel G. Fowle, W. W. Holden, and Charles B. Aycock are buried here.

Adjoining Oakwood is Raleigh's Hebrew Cemetery, organized in 1912 to augment the 1870 Hebrew section of Oakwood. A later bronze entrance tablet honors Jewish World War soldiers.

The John T. Turner house, 1002 Oberlin Road, is one of the oldest Oberlin Village houses still standing.

Reconstruction Era Villages

On the outskirts of Raleigh two villages were begun in
Reconstruction times. There is little left of the early Method settle-
ment, but a few of Oberlin Village's original houses remain.
According to the late historian W. G. Briggs, the blacks who bought
property were seeking two things: land of their own and education
for their children. James H. Harris, nationally prominent black
leader who served both as a Raleigh city alderman and as a
representative in the 1868 General Assembly, was one of the
promoters of Oberlin. Early purchasers included T. H. Williams,
who bought 1¾ acres for $90; James Shepard; Grandison Turner;
and Andrew Andrews, a black who drew a Confederate pension
for his labor in building the earth breastworks around the city in
1865. Oberlin residents organized a school for their children in
1869, seven years before Raleigh had a graded school system.

Another school, Latta University, was the ambitious project
of the Reverend M. L. Latta. One of its buildings still stands on
Parker Street. To solicit funds for his school, which was in operation
from 1892 to at least 1919, Latta traveled to Paris and London where
he had tea with Queen Victoria.

South of Hillsborough Street ex-slaves also purchased land
and settled the community called "Save-Rent," "The Little Place,"
and "Slab Town." It later became "Mason's Village," named for its
founder, Jesse Mason, and finally, Method. This community was
known for the Berry O'Kelly Training School, the first accredited
rural high school for blacks in North Carolina, and for its founder,
Berry O'Kelly.

Education

★ **Begin at the Capitol**
1 **Shaw University**
2 **Saint Augustine's College**
3 **Peace College**
4 **St. Mary's College**
5 **North Carolina State University**
6 **Meredith College**
7 **Research Triangle Park**

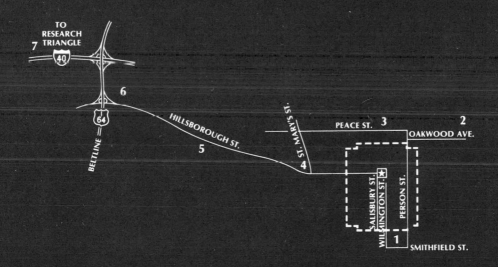

*Listed on the National Register of Historic Places and designated a Raleigh Historic Site.

Sculpture by Roy Gussow, School of Design garden

Shaw University

East South Street

Shaw University, chartered by the General Assembly in 1875 for the education of former slaves and their children, grew out of a small class begun in 1865 by Henry Martin Tupper who had been

Estey Hall, a landmark in black education, stands beside contemporary buildings on the Shaw University campus.

a chaplain in a Massachusetts regiment. In 1870 land was purchased at the south end of Fayetteville Street, using $5,000 of the $13,000 gift of Elijah J. Shaw, also of Massachusetts, for whom the school was later named. Students and faculty dug the clay, made the bricks, and felled the trees for timber to erect the first building, Shaw Hall, demolished in 1967.

In 1873 "Estey Seminary," named for another donor, Jacob Estey of Vermont, was built for women students. According to the Archives and History Survey report, "Estey Hall is a major landmark of south Raleigh .... as the oldest surviving building of Shaw University, it is one of the most important monuments of North Carolina's black history and is of particular significance in the history of the education of black women." Estey Hall is listed on the National Register of Historic Places and designated a Raleigh Historic Site. Many contemporary buildings have joined Estey Hall on the 21-acre Shaw campus and the university now has over 1,600 students.

Saint Augustine's College

Oakwood Avenue

In 1895 students of Saint Augustine's took stone from the quarry on campus and built a chapel which has two unusual features: a baptismal pool in addition to the usual Episcopal font; and a lich (or lych) gate, which Webster defines as "a roofed gate at the entrance to a churchyard where a coffin can be set down to await the arrival of the clergyman."

Saint Augustine's grew out of a class of four students who studied with the Reverend Jacob Brinton Smith. With contributions from Northern philanthropists, the Freedmen's Commission, and North Carolina Episcopalians, a tract of 30 acres was purchased and in 1867 Saint Augustine's Normal and Collegiate Institute was established by the Episcopal Church. The name was changed to Saint Augustine's College in 1928, and in 1934 the college became an accredited four-year, degree-granting institution.

Saint Augustine's has always been a liberal arts institution and once emphasized teacher training and preparation for the ministry. Saint Augustine officials estimate that one third of all black Episcopal clergymen attended or graduated from this college. The curriculum has changed to meet the needs of approximately 1,500 students. Currently engaged in a $30,000,000 revitalization program, the college has recently added six new buildings, making a total of 30 buildings on the 100-acre campus.

The lych gate is an unusual feature of the chapel at Saint Augustine's College.

Peace College

East Peace Street

    In 1872 Peace Institute, having been incorporated 14 years earlier, finally opened its doors and re-claimed its original purpose, "the thorough education of young ladies .... said school to be Presbyterian in its influence and course of education."

Main Building at Peace College is a lively center of student activity.

William Peace, an elder in the First Presbyterian Church, had given the land and $10,000 for a building which was partially completed when made available in 1862 for a Confederate hospital. No glass could be found for the windows, so painted muslin was attached to the frames to keep out the cold. After Raleigh's surrender in 1865, The Freedmen's Bureau took over the building.

In its early years Peace offered courses from kindergarten through college. Today Peace is a two-year college for women, owned by the First Presbyterian Church and operated by its own board of trustees. Twentieth century additions, which include seven new buildings since 1963, have been planned so that the original Greek Revival Main Building, listed on the National Register of Historic Places and designated a Raleigh Historic Site, retains its visual dominance.

St. Mary's College

900 Hillsborough Street

St. Mary's College was founded in 1842 by the Reverend Aldert Smedes on a campus which had originally been purchased by the Episcopal Diocese of North Carolina for a boys' school. When the school closed, Judge Duncan Cameron bought the property and later assisted Dr. Smedes in reopening it as St. Mary's School for Girls. In 1897 the Diocese of North Carolina purchased the property from the Cameron family.

The present 23-acre campus has 25 buildings, three of which date from the original boys' school. They are East Rock* and West Rock,* said to have been constructed of stone from the same quarry as that used in the building of the Capitol, and Smedes Hall.* The chapel,** given to St. Mary's in 1855 by the Cameron family, was designed by Richard Upjohn, architect of Christ Church in Raleigh and Trinity Church in New York City. In 1905 the transepts were added, giving the chapel its cruciform shape. This simple board and batten edifice is a fine example of Gothic Revival church architecture.

The St. Mary's College Chapel was built in 1855.

Today St. Mary's is a four-year institution offering courses ranging from the junior year of high school through the sophomore year of college. The school has about 520 students and 50 faculty members. Its board of trustees includes representatives from each of the five dioceses in North and South Carolina.

**Listed on the National Register of Historic Places and designated a Raleigh Historic Site.
*Designated a Raleigh Historic Site.

North Carolina State University

Hillsborough Street

A land-grant college, the North Carolina College of Agriculture and Mechanic Arts was established in 1889 on 62 acres given by R. Stanhope Pullen, who also gave land to the city for a park. Mr. Pullen led the mule that pulled a plow to divide the land given to the city and the college, and Pullen Road is part of that plow line. The first building, Holladay Hall, designated a Raleigh Historic Site, contained the whole college.

North Carolina State University now has 17,000 students, a faculty of 1,200, and 120 buildings on its 596-acre campus. With extension offices and programs in each of North Carolina's 100 counties, the university also maintains research stations, camps, and thousands of acres of forest and other properties.

One of the foremost institutions in the nation for granting Ph.D.'s in science and engineering, North Carolina State University offers course work in 70 fields. Its School of Design, established in 1948 by Henry L. Kamphoefner, is internationally known and attracts outstanding faculty and students from all over the world.

D. H. Hill Library and circular Harrelson Hall overlook the plaza called the "brick yard" on the North Carolina State University campus.

McIver Amphitheater and gardens at Meredith College are enjoyed by all.

Meredith College

Hillsborough Street

Meredith College began its life in 1899 as the Baptist Female University which in 1909 became Meredith College. When in 1889 the Baptist State Convention voted to establish the institution, it was hoped that the school could open its doors with a campus of at least eight acres and an endowment of $50,000. It opened 10 years later on one-fourth of a city square, next door to the Executive Mansion, with a debt of $35,000.

The college soon outgrew its Blount Street address and it was moved during the Christmas vacation of 1925-1926 to its present site of 225 acres. Students and faculty of that year remember vividly the move. The mud was so deep that the *Twig* editor wrote, "The new Meredith seemed, like Venice, to be built in the sea; but this is a sea of mud."

Through the years, the college, stressing the preeminence of academic integrity and spiritual influence, has continued to grow with over 1,200 full-time students and approximately 200 enrolled in the Continuing Education program. The campus has 23 buildings with others being constructed.

Contemporary Writing in Raleigh

North Carolina's great native son, playwright Paul Green, said that when he went from Harnett County to Chapel Hill in the years just before World War I he had never seen a man who had written a book. But there was one man in Chapel Hill who had; and, said Green, "they used to point him out to people, to visitors, as a man who had written a book." That man was Dr. Archibald Henderson, noted mathematician and biographer of George Bernard Shaw.

The same thing may have applied in Raleigh in those years. There were not many men or women around who had written a book. There were some who had brought out private works of poems or reminiscences. Judge William Gaston had dabbled in poetry, and

Dr. Calvin Wiley had edited the *North Carolina Reader* in the mid 1800s. But the blossoming of the literary arts did not come until later.

When Primrose McPherson drew the first Literary Map of North Carolina, the writer she selected to depict Raleigh was Jonathan Daniels, and Daniels is shown perched atop the Capitol dome looking out of a telescope. Daniels and his father, Josephus Daniels, did write books — many of them — and in those years of the 1920s and 1930s several others became known as writers. Ann Bridgers wrote a play, "Coquette," which was produced on Broadway, and some members of the faculty at North Carolina State became authors of academic work.

It was from North Carolina State that the real impetus for creative writing came in the 1950s and 1960s. Novelist and Poet Guy Owen brought his now nationally known *Southern Poetry Review* to the campus when he joined the English faculty and he has continued to write and to encourage others to write. Out of the Writers Workshop at North Carolina State there were at last count 16 books which have been written. Romulus Linney was the first writer-in-residence on the campus; but before him there had been writers such as Lodwick Hartley, Richard Walser and others, and it is Walser who has done more than anyone else in the state to arouse interest in North Carolina writers.

Sally Buckner has done much to stir the creative sparks at Peace College, and today there are several groups of writers who gather regularly to read and discuss their works. Among them are the Longview Writers, and at one time the very fine Longview literary magazine was published. Other sessions have been held at Olivia Raney Library.

Among those who are regularly producing books are Peggy Hoffmann, Ben Haas, Charlotte Hilton Green, Helen Tucker, and many others, such as Linda Grimsley, Thomas Walters, Gerald Barra, Jack Kearins and Betty Adcock, who are authors of published works.

Creative writing classes continue at North Carolina State, at Peace and other colleges in the city, and the works of dozens of writers appear regularly in magazines across the state, South and nation. The literary arts have not only burgeoned but are flourishing.

Sam Ragan

Sam Ragan is editor of the *Southern Pines Pilot*.

Research Triangle Park

"The Research Triangle is an idea that has produced a reality — the idea that the scientific brains and research talents of .... three institutions, and their life of research in many fields, could provide the background and stimulation of research for the benefit of the state and nation. In a way, the Research Triangle is the marriage of North Carolina's ideals for higher education and its hopes for material progress." (Luther H. Hodges, *Businessman in the Statehouse: Six Years as Governor of North Carolina*, 1962.) In 1955 Governor Hodges envisioned the Research Triangle as a possible solution to the problem of the low wage-scale of principal North Carolina industries. The establishment of the park has brought together leaders of the universities, state government, industry, and financial organizations.

Since it opened in 1959 with one organization and 20 people, the 5400-acre Research Triangle Park, largest research park in the nation, has grown to 21 research organizations with a total of 10,000 employees, over half of them living in Raleigh.

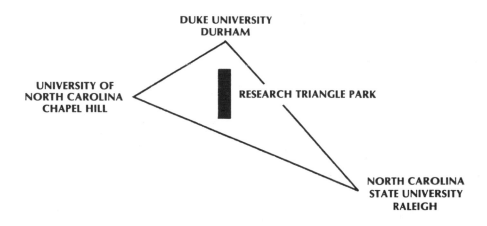

Activities

★ Begin at the Capitol
1 Olivia Raney Library
2 Chavis Park
3 Pullen Park
4 Stewart Theatre
5 Reynolds Coliseum
6 Thompson Theatre
7 Theatre in the Park

8 Raleigh Little Theatre
   Raleigh Rose Garden
9 Dorton Arena*
10 Carter Stadium
11 Raleigh Woman's Club Garden

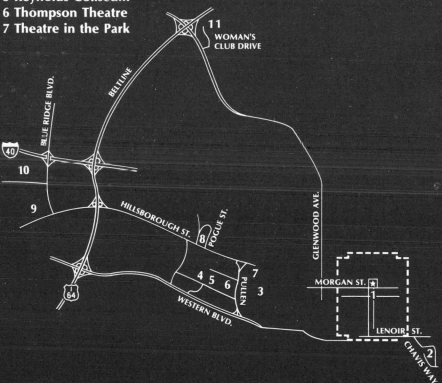

*Listed on the National Register of Historic Places and designated a Raleigh Historic Site.

Friends of the College performance

J. S. Dorton Arena

North Carolina State Fairgrounds
West Hillsborough Street

Once humorously known as the "Cow Palace," the J. S. Dorton Arena, built by the North Carolina Department of Agriculture as a live-stock judging pavilion, houses many activities and events, including dog shows, horse shows, and musical entertainment.

Dorton Arena, a "paraboleum," is an internationally famous prototype of a parabolic suspension structure. The revolutionary

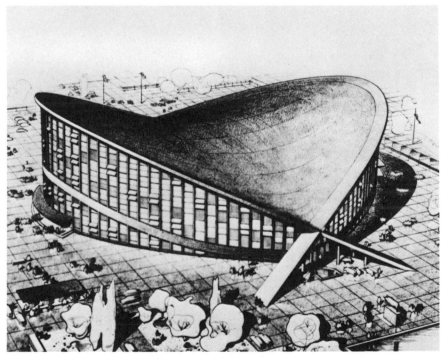

Matthew Nowicki's drawing shows the development of his design for Dorton Arena.

expanse of uninterrupted space inside the arena is the result of a rare integration of architecture and engineering. The building has received world-wide recognition and numerous awards, including the American Institute of Architects' First Honor Award in 1953.

The innovative design of Dorton Arena, one of the earliest examples of the combination of the forces of tension and compression in architecture, was conceived by Matthew Nowicki (pronounced No-vit-ski), a Polish immigrant. Nowicki, a member of the Allied Underground during the Russian invasion of Poland in World War II, helped lay out the new capital city of Warsaw and assisted in the design of the United Nations complex.

Nowicki later became associated with the North Carolina State College School of Design and worked with the late William Henley Deitrick, Raleigh architect, in designing the State Fair complex. When Nowicki was killed in a plane crash in 1950, his plan was carried out with only minimal changes by Deitrick's firm, and the arena was built under a state appropriation of $1,500,000. Dedicated in 1953, it was called the Livestock Judging Pavilion until 1961 when its name was changed to honor long-time fair manager, J. S. Dorton.

Sports in Raleigh

Lovers of sports — both as participants and spectators — find many things in Raleigh for their pleasure.

All of the junior and senior high schools have well-rounded programs as do the six colleges in the city. The City Recreation Department offers organized competition for all ages in a variety of sports. The YMCA and YWCA facilities are superb, as are those of various community clubs that feature swimming pools and tennis courts. Thousands of Raleigh boys and girls participate in a wide variety of swimming programs conducted under expert instruction.

Activities are geared to the non-professional participant, but the television stations that serve the area are aware of the strong interest in all sports and bring all of the major professional events via their media.

North Carolina State provided the national collegiate basketball champion of 1974, and its 12,400-capacity Reynolds Coliseum is sold out for almost every home game of the Wolfpack. So is its 45,000-capacity Carter Stadium — one of the best in the nation — for football. The N. C. State baseball team is one of the strongest in college ranks and admits spectators to its games without charge.

Shaw University also provides collegiate football and basketball for men, and Saint Augustine's has a strong men's college basketball team. Sports for women on an intercollegiate level are growing rapidly.

Weather and facilities for golf are ideal with a wide variety of courses available in the city and many more within a few miles. Raleigh is a regular stop on the Ladies Professional Golf Association Tour. The Raleigh Racquet Club is frequent host for the

The State-Carolina game always draws capacity crowds to Carter Stadium.

Southern Tennis Championships. Bowlers have adequate alleys for their sport.

The annual Lions Horse Show is one of the largest in the country. It is held at Dorton Arena, a unique 9,000-seat indoor stadium.

City owned Lake Wheeler provides boating and fishing, and Kerr Lake and Gaston Lake, major impoundments, are within an hour's drive. Raleigh residents can be at the ocean in two to three hours, and numerous winter ski resorts can be reached in four hours of careful driving. Many types of hunting also are available close by.

The sportsman and sports spectator enjoy living in Raleigh.

Dick Herbert

Dick Herbert is Public Relations Director, American Football Coaches Association.

Theatre in Raleigh

Raleigh supports a wealth of professional, semi-professional, and amateur theatre far beyond its size. During almost any week of the year, one has the opportunity to see live drama ranging from the classics to contemporary experimental plays.

The principal theatres which are continually either in production or rehearsal are Stewart Theatre on the NCSU campus, the Raleigh Little Theatre, Theatre in the Park, and Thompson Theatre also at NCSU. All of the other college campuses in town mount a limited but effective drama season. These include Meredith, Peace, St. Mary's, Saint Augustine's, and Shaw.

The Stewart Theatre, with its 850 seats and an excellent stage, presents professional American and European touring groups at a moderate cost. Each year companies like the City Center Acting Company and the Royal Shakespeare bring Raleigh the best of classic and modern drama. Moreover, Stewart Theatre books outstanding Broadway musicals which play in Memorial Auditorium. Besides its scheduled drama series, Stewart remains in continuous use with a rich fare of student sponsored touring groups which are ridiculously inexpensive.

The Raleigh Little Theatre, located on Pogue Street, is a community theatre with a strong following. Its season usually includes five productions of both musicals and recognized modern drama. Not only does it provide respectable theatre, but it also encourages community participation at all levels of production. At various times during the year, it conducts workshops in all phases of theatre for both youth and adult classes.

Theatre in the Park, located in Pullen Park near the Bell Tower, is also a community theatre offering strong productions at a minimal cost. With casts ranging from young people to adults, Theatre in the Park produces both classics and experimental productions. It too offers regular workshops in theatre, dance, and puppetry. It houses Raleigh's only puppet theatre. Under the direction of North Carolina School of the Arts graduates, it has annually toured original productions in the North Carolina school system.

Thompson Theatre is the student theatre on the NCSU campus where contemporary, experimental, and classic theatre is produced under the direction of a professional staff. Each school year three major productions are staged. Between major shows Thompson has a series of workshop productions which are almost always sold out by performance time.

Michael S. Reynolds is an associate professor at North Carolina State University.

Stewart Theatre
University Student Center
North Carolina State University
Cates Avenue off Pullen Road.
Information: 737-3105

Raleigh Little Theater
301 Pogue Street
Information: 821-3111

Thompson Theatre
North Carolina State University
Dunn Street off Pullen Road
Information: 737-2405

Pullen Theatre in the Park
105 Pullen Road
Information: 755-6058

Music in Raleigh

Raleigh has become the "Athens of the Southeast" in the field of music. Three large concert series, with single tickets available for two of them, provide exposure to the finest individual musicians and to both small and large ensembles whose reputations are already established worldwide.

Elsewhere you will read of Raleigh's newly acquired North Carolina Symphony, with its cadre of young musicians accompanying such greats as soprano Phyllis Curtin, violinist Eugene Fodor, and trumpeter Doc Severinson. Conductor John Gosling encompasses all kinds of music!

Mention pop concert and one slides easily into Ella Fitzgerald and Count Basie, billed without exaggeration as the height of the Stewart Theatre musical series, and to the rock, soul, country, and gospel groups which ease in and out of town frequently, often at North Carolina State University.

Friends of the College is known all over the world as a mammoth series at a most modest fee. Held at North Carolina State University's Reynolds Coliseum, the series relies on large ensembles, such as The Chinese Folk Dancers and Acrobats, the Moscow State Symphony Orchestra, Boris Goldovsky's Grand Opera Theatre, and the London Symphony Orchestra.

Name the opera and one is reminded of the National Opera Company which headquarters in Raleigh and provides an opportunity to hear the most promising young singers on the way up. Or name the Pittsburgh Ballet Theatre on the "Friends" series and glide gracefully into the Stewart Theatre's five dance programs ranging from classical ballet to modern, to Spanish, to African dance.

The North Carolina Museum of Art presents rising young soloists and small groups as part of its educational program. Mention education and you are face to face with the Raleigh Music Club, an organization open to music lovers, which sponsors scholarship contests for young musicians.

In a similar category are the student master class and student festival promoted each year by the Raleigh Chamber Music

Guild. This organization presents the third prestigious series with such top performers as the Tokyo and Amati string quartets, the Festival Winds, and the Piedmont Chamber Orchestra.

In addition, the Raleigh Oratorio Society exposes Raleigh to great choral music, as do the many local churches with their fine choirs and superior organists. Organ recitals in these same churches and in Raleigh's six colleges and universities are often heard on the music series of each of these institutions — this, in addition to their solo, choral, and instrumental student performers.

There is something for everyone's taste. One hardly needs to roam as far as Chapel Hill or Durham to supplement the diet. It is all here in Raleigh for the feasting.

Nell Hirschberg

Nell Hirschberg is music critic for the *News & Observer.*

The Magic Merry-Go-Round

The merry-go-round's rabbits had straight pink ears and the horses stared from wild, unseeing eyes. The man, who always wore a straw hat, took your ticket and you raced to your favorite animal. Then the man cranked up the machinery, the music played, and the animals went up and down, up and down.

The music is different now and the location has changed, but the animals in the Pullen Park carousel are the same ones that have carried at least three generations of Raleigh children. The wooden animals, hand-carved and polychromed, are attributed to Salvatore Cernigliaro for the Dentzel Carousel Company of Philadelphia, Pennsylvania (1903-1909) whose work is represented in the Abby Aldrich Rockefeller Museum of Folk Art in Williamsburg, Virginia. The Smithsonian Institution also has a Dentzel carousel.

The merry-go-round was acquired from Bloomsbury Park, the short-lived mecca at the end of the streetcar line, where it had been installed in 1912. The park covered 100 acres (now the Carolina Country Club and Country Club Hills) and also had a roller coaster, a penny arcade, and a dancing pavilion.

Gardens in Raleigh

In addition to the previously mentioned gardens at the Legislative Building, the Ellen Mordecai Garden at Mordecai Historic Park, and the garden planned for the Joel Lane house, Capitol Square has trees that are labeled and beds of seasonal flowers. The following gardens are also open to the public:

The **AIA Courtyard,** 115 West Morgan Street, enclosed by a brick wall, is planted with liriope, pachysandra, evergreen shrubs, and a large catalpa tree.

The Mary Lee McMillan Garden, at the **Raleigh Woman's Club,** 3300 Woman's Club Drive, was a gift of the Raleigh Garden Club. The plantings include azaleas, camellias, dogwood, winter blooming cherries, and ajuga.

WRAL-TV Studio, 2619 Western Boulevard, maintains a spring garden with flowering fruit trees, azaleas, and rhododendrons.

Chapel Garden on the grounds of **Dorothea Dix Hospital,** South Boylan Avenue, was a gift of the Garden Club of North Carolina to provide both therapy and pleasure for the patients. It contains unusual plants such as plume poppy, cruel vine, and large sasanqua camellias.

The Raleigh Rose Garden, 301 Pogue Street, features an arbor with climbing roses as well as beds of roses.

The water garden on U. S. 70 West at Bell Design Group is part of a landscaped area with a lake.

Peace College has a beautiful area behind its Main Building, and **Meredith College** has an unusual Lake Amphitheater with landscaping of azaleas and spring shrubs.

At **North Carolina State University,** the Gardner Arboretum features a planting of old roses; the School of Design Garden contains sculpture by Roy Gussow; the Conservatory, which is open to the public on weekdays except Tuesdays, has a collection of tropical and subtropical plants; and the Method Test Garden on Method Road, open daily, has seasonal color with roses, azaleas, and summer flowers.

Hundreds of varieties of roses are identified in the Raleigh Rose Garden.

Parks and Recreation

Raleigh now has 108 open spaces and permanent parks, the largest of them being Pullen Park and Chavis Park, named for R. Stanhope Pullen who gave the land to the city in 1887 and John Chavis, black leader and educator of pre-Civil War times.

In addition to Pullen and Chavis parks, some of the properties maintained and operated by the Raleigh Parks and Recreation Department include 18 community centers, mini-parks throughout the city, the Raleigh Rose Garden, and Nash and Moore Squares.

The following recreational facilities are available, with swimming pools open from May 31 - September 1 and amusement rides in operation from March 15 - December 1.

Pullen Park, Western Boulevard
Information: 755-6468
Swimming pool; lighted, all-weather tennis courts; ball fields; picnic areas; amusement rides

Arts & Crafts Center, 105 Pullen Road
Information: 755-6126
Year-round classes for adults

Pullen Theatre in the Park, 105 Pullen Road
Information: 755-6058
Entertainment and instruction in the performing arts

Chavis Park, Holmes Avenue
Information: 755-6989
Swimming pool, all-weather tennis courts, ball fields, picnic areas, merry-go-round

Pullen Theatre in the Park, sponsored by the Raleigh Parks and Recreation Department, is a community center for all the performing arts.

How Would You Like to Live Here?

Raleigh, one of 12 cities in the nation that has been honored with the All-American City Award for citizen participation in city government, is a pleasant place to visit — but how would you like to live here? Raleigh has four seasons and a mild climate, with a normal temperature range from the low 30s to the low 50s in the winter. The average summertime temperature falls in the upper 80s.

With a population of 145,000, Raleigh is the fourth largest city in the state. The average household income is over $14,000, making this city one of the most affluent in the Southeast.

If you lived in Raleigh, you would be protected by a uniformed and sworn police force of 307, plus seven uniformed and sworn Park Rangers with the same training and authority. There are 14 fire stations and approximately 322 firemen. You would have a choice of over 180,000 books in nine branches of the Wake County Libraries.

City and county schools are merging, but Raleigh currently provides 33 public schools with a total enrollment of over 20,000 and a teacher/pupil ratio of approximately 22. Raleigh is a center of education with six colleges and universities.

The city's growth has been matched by the addition of shopping centers. The earliest of them, Cameron Village, dates from 1949. North Hills Mall and Crabtree Valley Mall are the largest.

Raleigh has grown from its original 400 acres, less than a square mile, in 1792 to over 51 square miles in 1975. Two of its original squares, Moore and Nash, are still available for your use. Facing Moore Square, the City Market stands almost empty during the week; but on Saturdays its stalls are loaded with flowers and home-grown vegetables for sale. Raleigh has parks which cover a total of 2,500 acres of land and water. Even with 518 miles of paved streets, Raleigh has remained the City of Oaks.

State Government Visitor Center*

301 North Blount Street
Information: 829-3456

A Visitor Center for the State Capital Complex will open in 1976 in the state-owned Andrews-London house. The center will schedule tours of state buildings, including the Capitol, Legislative Building, Executive Mansion, and the state museums. Orientation programs will be provided for school children and leaflets, brochures, and other information will be available.

*A ramp is provided for physically handicapped visitors.

Credits

Design by Mary Holdt/Ferree Studios
Cover Poem by Ardis Kimzey
Cover Art by Joe Cox

Art:
Annette Marsland 18, 19
Edwin F. Harris, Jr. 24, 25
Pete Turner 46
Betty Eichenberger 50
Walt Obman 90

Photography:
Gordon H. Schenck, Jr. 8, 10, 13, 20, 23, 26, 28, 35, 37, 38, 41, 48,
                        52, 54, 56, 58, 63, 64, 66, 68, 70, 73, 75, 77
North Carolina Museum of History 7, 31, 84, 97
North Carolina Museum of Art 32
Lewis Clarke Associates 42
North Carolina Symphony 45
News & Observer — Raleigh Times 61, 95
Saint Augustine's College 72
Bill Norton 78
Friends of the College 82
North Carolina State University
   Athletic Department 86
Gus Martin 93

        More than 100 Raleigh Fine Arts Society volunteers have participated in the prep-
aration, production, and distribution of this book. In addition to the work of its
own members, the Raleigh Fine Arts Society appreciates the assistance of the North
Carolina Department of Cultural Resources, the English Department and School of
Design of North Carolina State University, the Society for the Preservation of Historic
Oakwood, the North Carolina Chapter of the American Institute of Architects, and
the North Carolina Bicentennial.

Index

Sources

Architectural details and much of the historical information used in descriptions of buildings on the National Register of Historic Places were obtained from the Survey Branch, Historic Sites Section, Division of Archives and History.

In addition to local newspapers of the period, including the *News and Observer* and *Raleigh Times*, sources used in the preparation of this book included the following:

Moses N. Amis, *Historical Raleigh* (Raleigh: Commercial Printing Co., 1913)

Hope Summerell Chamberlain, *History of Wake County* (Raleigh: Edwards and Broughton, 1922)

Bertha Maye Edwards, *The Little Place and the Little Girl* (New York: Carlton Press, 1974)

Marshall De Lancey Haywood, *Builders of the Old North State*, co   d by Mattie Bailey Haywood and edited by Sarah McCulloh Lemmon, (Raleigh: Litho Industries, 1968)

Rev. Morgan London Latta, *Story of My Life and Work* (Raleigh: Edwards and Broughton, 1903)

Hugh Lefler, *North Carolina History Told by Contemporaries* (Chapel Hill: University of North Carolina Press, 1934)

Elizabeth Davis Reid, *From Raleigh's Past* (Raleigh: Branch Banking and Trust Co., 1965)

Marguerite E. Schumann, *Strolling at State* (Raleigh: North Carolina State University Alumni Association, Inc., 1973)

Walter M. Stearns, *Haywood Hall* (Raleigh: Wake County Committee of the North Carolina Society of the Colonial Dames of America, 1948)

David Lowry Swain, *The Centennial Celebration of Raleigh* (Raleigh: Edwards and Broughton, 1893)

David Lowry Swain, *Early Times in Raleigh*, compiled by R. S. Tucker, (Raleigh: Walters, Hughes, and Co., 1867)

Elizabeth Culbertson Waugh, *North Carolina's Capital, Raleigh* (Raleigh: The Junior League of Raleigh, Inc. and the Raleigh Historic Sites Commission, Inc., 1967)

Charlotte Bryan (Grimes) Williams, *History of the Wake County Ladies Memorial Association* (Raleigh: 1938)

The State, Vol. 3, April 18, 1936; Vol. 17, Nov. 5, 1949

Ben F. Williams, "A Visit to Possagno," *North Carolina Museum of Art Bulletin*, Vol. I, numbers 4 and 5, 1957-1958.

Mrs. Marshall De Lancey Haywood, *Life in the Richest Era — Late 1800s and early 1900s*, interview recorded by a Junior Historian Club

Reminiscences of Oakwood Residents, recorded by a history class under the direction of Sarah McCulloh Lemmon